DEDICATION

This book is dedicated with the deepest respect and love to my grandmother, Sadie Ruby. Sadie loved embroidery and passed her passion on to me. I am also dedicating this to my wonderful Scott, for his unlimited enthusiasm and support for my adventures in art and embroidery.

ACKNOWLEDGMENTS

Special thanks to the following for their contributions of materials: Dritz, Gerald and Two Hands Paperie, Golden Acrylic Paints, and Luz De Luna. Enormous thanks to Linda Leibovich, Purna Hegde, and Sasha Schlesinger for contributing their talents and feedback. Thanks to my family for the encouragement—Alex and Marcia Eisner, Jason Reinin, and Sasha and Noah Schlesinger.

Thanks to all the staff at C&T Publishing, including Zinnia Heinzmann; my special editors Roxane Cerda, Liz Aneloski, and Kathryn Patterson; and photographers Rachel Holmes, Diane Pedersen, Kelly Burgoyne, and Estefany Gonzalez.

CONTENTS

artful Embroidery on Canvas

GET CREATIVE WITH THREAD, FABRIC, PAPER, ACRYLIC MEDIUMS & MORE

Irene Schlesinger

INSPIRE

C&T PUBLISHING

Text copyright © 2020 by Irene Schlesinger

Photography and artwork copyright © 2020 by C&T Publishing, Inc.

Publisher: Amy Barrett-Daffin

Creative Director: Gailen Runge

Acquisitions Editor: Roxane Cerda

Managing Editor: Liz Aneloski

Editor: Kathryn Patterson

Technical Editor: Debbie Rodgers

Cover/Book Designer: April Mostek

Production Coordinator: Tim Manibusan

Production Editor: Alice Mace Nakanishi

Illustrator: Linda Johnson

Photo Assistant: Rachel Holmes

Subjects photography by Rachel Holmes and Diane Pedersen and instructional photography by Kelly Burgoyne and Estefany Gonzalez of C&T Publishing, Inc., unless otherwise noted

Published by C&T Publishing, Inc., P.O. Box 1456, Lafayette, CA 94549

Library of Congress Control Number:2019946321

Printed in the USA

10 9 8 7 6 5 4 3 2 1

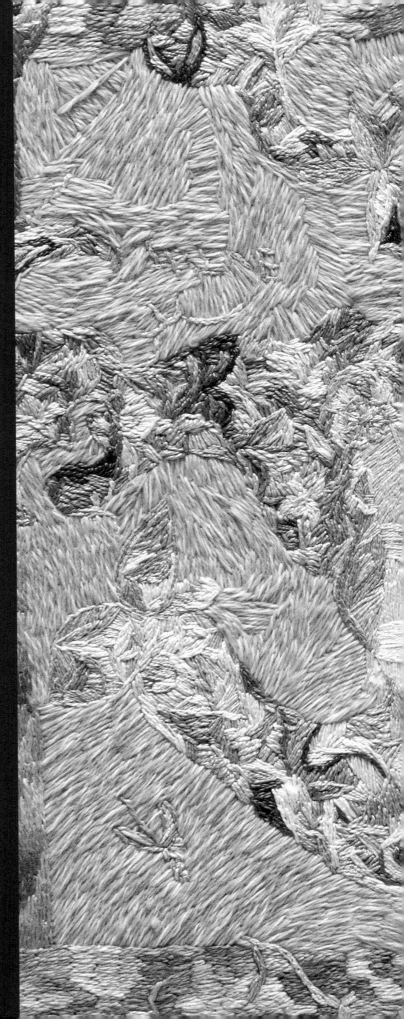

Stitching on Canvas

Embroidering on stretched canvas can be as pleasurable as stitching with a hoop. Stretched canvas has a smooth, taut surface waiting for you and your big needles. This opening chapter is provided to acquaint the needlework beginner with the few basic stitches for completing the projects included in the book.

The projects are open-ended. The more advanced embroiderer could and should switch them up by adding more elaborate stitching. The stitches that follow are not difficult; practice will lead to mastering them. Mastering them will lead to improvising, which is a path to developing your own unique style.

In your hands, a needle becomes a paintbrush. Your stitches are as unique as the strokes from an artist's brush. As artists, we want to be unique, original, and memorable.

RUNNING AND DOUBLE RUNNING STITCH

Running stitches are (traditionally) uniform straight stitches with uniform spaces between. I outline areas with a running stitch and then go back and fill the spaces between the stitches. That is known as a *double running stitch*.

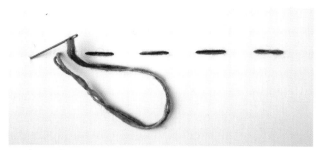
Traditional running stitch

Double running stitch

STEM STITCH

The *stem stitch* is also used for lines and outlining. The first stitch is a straight stitch. The needle comes up through the canvas and then goes back down into the canvas. The next stitch starts alongside the middle of the first stitch … and *sew* it goes.

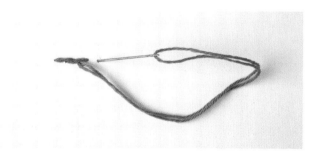
Stem stitch

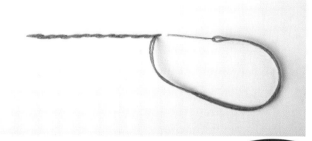
Row of stem stitches

SATIN STITCH

The *satin stitch* is used for filling in spaces and shapes. It's a series of straight stitches that line up next to each other.

TIP || *To keep long satin stitches from catching on something, use a glue stick on the area of the canvas that the stitches will cover. This keeps the yarn in place. (Be sure to use a glue stick—using a wet glue will gunk it up.)*

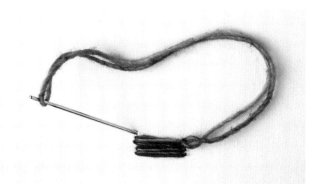
Satin stitches

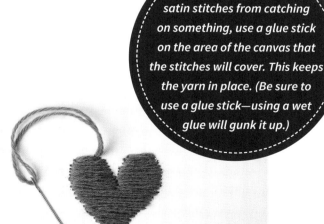
Satin-stitched heart

SIMPLIFIED SHISHA STITCH

The *shisha stitch* is one method of attaching small flat objects, such as mirrors or mosaic tiles, to your canvas. I am showing you a mini version of this stitch and also another option for adding these items to the canvas. Before I stitch the mirror, I glue it into place. This prevents the mirror from sliding around while I'm stitching. I'm using different colors of thread so you may see each step more clearly.

The first part is creating a frame over the mirror using four straight stitches.

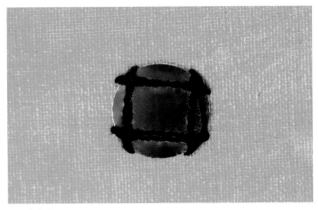

Box it in!

Next, using straight stitches, create a diamond to further lock the mirror in.

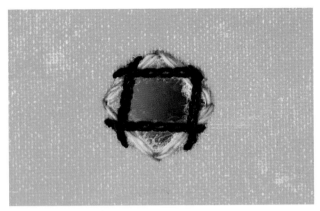

Add diagonal stitches.

Pull the needle up in a corner, then pull it under the two yarns that are part of the square and diamond outlines.

Secure corners.

That's all it takes!

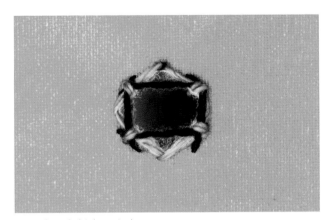

Completed shisha stitch

Begin by gluing the mirror to a piece of scrap paper that is a little bigger than the mirror. When it is dry, attach it onto the canvas with craft glue. Be careful with glue—it can mess up the mirror, and that's no fun!

Attach with glue.

When the mirror on the paper is firmly attached to the canvas, stitch on the paper surrounding the mirror. Running stitches will become double running stitches to hide the paper and keep the mirror attached to the canvas.

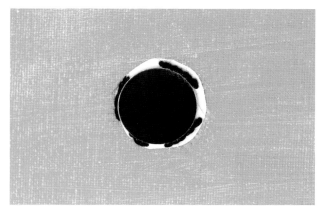

Stitch to the canvas.

Go around a few times. If you don't want the edges of the mirror to show, go back and bring the needle as close as you can to the edge of the mirror, and build up the yarn until it's above the mirror. Stitching over stitches makes this happen. Be sure the mirror is firmly attached with glue before stitching.

Build the yarn up to cover the edges.

ADDING SEQUINS

For the *Calavera* project (page 30), you may desire to add sequins and beaded sequins to the canvas. Here's a quick look at a way to add these. This process is not hard at all. You will be able to sequin up your world!

Sequins and beads should be stitched on. Use a regular sewing needle and thread. Make sure there is a knot at the end of the thread. Sequins should be sewn concave side up.

Position the sequin.

Bring the needle up next to the sequin, then stitch into the hole of the sequin.

Bring the needle up on the other side of the sequin, then return it to the hole.

The sequin is now attached. Go to the back of the canvas, tie a knot and leave a longish thread tail.

BEADED SEQUINS

If you are adding beads atop the sequins, you may need to use a beading needle with beading thread for those supersmall seed beads. A regular sewing needle is usually small enough to pass through larger beads.

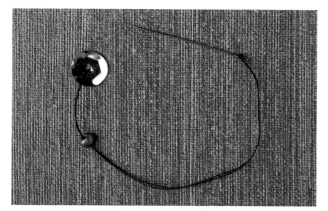

Using beading thread on a regular sewing needle, make a knot on the end of the thread, come up through the canvas into the sequin, and then through the bead.

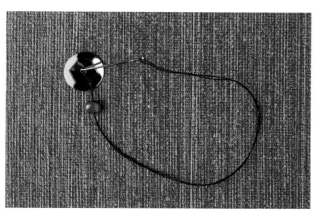

Return the needle into the sequin and the canvas. When you go back through the hole in the sequin, try to avoid going back into the same hole in the canvas that you created when pulling the thread up. Create a new hole.

Beaded sequin

Starting Out:
Notes on Supplies

CANVAS

For the projects in this book, we are using 12″ × 12″ (30.5 cm × 30.5 cm) stretched canvases with staples in the back. The canvas to look for is medium-weight cotton duck. Anything thicker will be hard on your hands to stitch through. The canvas surface should be taut.

Cover the edges and sides of the canvas with masking tape. This will protect the part of the canvas that will be exposed after you have finished your piece, leaving it clean and fingerprint-free.

If you are using a canvas with staples on the sides, you can cover the staples (if you wish) with white gaffer's tape. Gaffer's tape is a heavy, cotton cloth, pressure-sensitive tape that looks and feels like canvas. If it is unavailable at your local art store, it can often be found at a hardware store.

Protect the edges of your stretched canvas with masking tape.

NEEDLES

Look for two features in the needles you will be using on canvas:

• A sharp, pointed needle that will effortlessly pierce and go through the canvas

• A needle with an eye that is large and long enough to pull threads, flosses, and yarns easily through the canvas

Needles that have these features are sold as darners, yarn darners, European darners, chenille, and crewel/embroidery. Have a variety on hand. Practice using them to determine what feels good in your hand. Other needles to consider adding to your toolbox are regular sewing needles, sharps, beading, and appliqué needles.

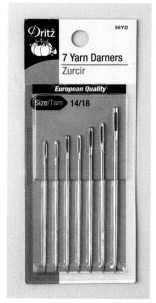

Invest in a variety of needles.

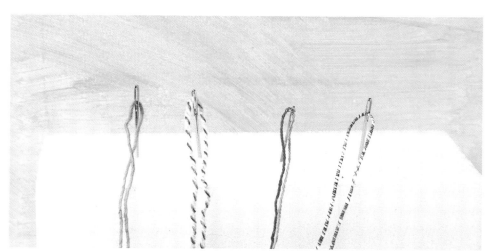

I use Styrofoam blocks to hold my threaded needles.

THREAD, FLOSS, AND YARN

Any fiber that will easily fit through the eye of a needle and can be flexed and bent can be used. Yarn or thread with a bumpy texture can tear the canvas. Textured yarns can be frustrating to stitch with and can cause the yarn to fray and split up. The key is to be sure the needle has a larger circumference than the yarn. Practice stitching any questionable-textured yarn on a practice canvas with a needle. Go slow when stitching with textured yarns. Should a bit of the canvas tear, you can repair it by removing the stitch that caused the problem, covering the tear with a piece of masking tape, and starting again. Try again, or consider trading that yarn for a smoother yarn.

Use a large needle and stitch slowly when using bumpy yarn.

ADDITIONAL SUPPLIES

• An extra canvas to practice on

• Scissors and snippers

• 12″ (30.5 cm) ruler

• Camera or phone to take reference pictures

• Tape, 1″ (2.5 cm)-wide masking or artist's tape

• Glue in glue stick form (any type)

• Tacky or craft glue

• Jewel glue, such as E-6000

• Options for design, such as clip art
(*Note: If you want to use someone else's artwork, be sure the copyright allows you to do so and that you follow all guidelines associated with the copyright.*)

• Inkjet-printable fabric sheets

• Butcher or packaging paper

• Household glue, such as Elmer's Glue-All

• Small eye screws (2 per canvas)

• About 30″ (76.2 cm) of picture framing wire for each canvas under 5 pounds (2.27 kg)

• A small water spritzer or sponge

Thoughts on Design

The visual weight of the items in a picture or composition and how the items are placed can create a balanced, visually pleasing art piece. Parts of the projects included in this book are left open-ended for you to individualize your canvas. Here are some basic design formations to consider as you plan your compositions.

SYMMETRICAL, ASYMMETRICAL, AND RADIAL DESIGNS

Symmetry occurs when the sides of a composition are equally balanced.

An asymmetrical design is when the sides of a design are not equally balanced.

In a radial composition, items are arranged in a circular way.

PATTERNS

Patterns are simply recurring designs.

ARRANGING ELEMENTS OF VISUAL WEIGHT

"Arranging elements of visual weight" is a way of saying, "It's time to compose the picture on your canvas." Bring out all the items that have inspired you to create this piece. Gather the patterns, yarns, fabric, paper, and embellishments that you may decide to use.

Begin by deciding if the background will be painted, papered, or have fabric attached to the canvas. Will you stitch in the uncovered areas (also known as *negative space*) later?

Once the background has been decided, place your patterns and embellishments on your canvas and move them around until you find a composition that feels good to you. If you have trouble, try arranging the items in one of the design formations previously defined. Check out some of the Elements of Inspiration (page 18). Take pictures or write notes on the composition so you can refer back to it as you create the canvas.

COLORS—WARM AND COOL

Colors create mood and are often described as warm or cool.

Colors perceived as warm are those associated with heat, such as reds, oranges, golds, egg-yolk yellow, and some browns. Warm colors tend to come forward.

Cool colors, such as blues, greens, lemon yellow, and some grays, tend to recede.

Elements of Inspiration

Detail of *Safe Space* (full image on page 58)

Artful Embroidery on Canvas

NOTES ON INSPIRATION

There is much to be inspired by, and there are many ways to bring that inspiration to the canvas. Photographs, writing, and other two-dimensional mementos may all be included via a printer and the printable fabric sheet of your choice. An increasing variety of inkjet printable fabrics are becoming available. Inkjet sheets are available in cotton, silk, organza, cotton poplin, and other types of fabrics. I advise making copies of any treasured photos or papers and saving the originals among your keepsakes, as mistakes can happen.

I printed out this photo of Grandma Betsy and Dad by using an inkjet printable fabric sheet.

Is there an image you are thinking of, but you are unable to create on your own? Chances are you will find what you need with clip art. Clip art is available online and also in book form. Just be aware that not all clip art images are free. Some images are copyright-free, but others have strict copyright guidelines about how they're used, number of times used, whether they're for resale, crediting, requiring written permission, and so on. *If you want to use someone else's artwork, be sure the copyright allows you to do so and that you follow all guidelines associated with the copyright.*

PAPER AND FABRIC

An inspiring feature of creating on canvas is using assorted papers and fabrics with stitchery. The variety of papers and fabrics is vast, and that is excellent for inspiration and for crafting. Stretched canvas offers a firm base for stitching on papers. When choosing papers and fabrics, consider how the needle will work with the material and go through the canvas. For instance, if you are working with kraft-tex—a vegan leather alternative (by C&T Publishing)—you may wish to prepunch holes to make it easier to stitch through. I have addressed working with thick and fragile materials in the *Start with a Heart* project (page 24). With paper and some fabrics, do test a piece of the material if you are planning to use glue or any of the acrylic mediums with it. Sometimes moisture will cause the dye in a material to leak, bleed, or buckle the paper or fabric. You want to know about that before you continue.

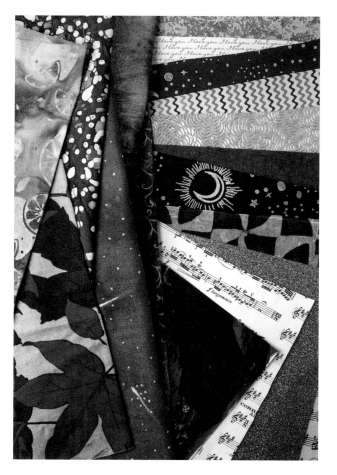

BEADS, EMBELLISHMENTS, *MILAGROS*, AND MIRRORS

Beads, embellishments, *milagros*, charms, bells, sequins, ribbons, and other bits of this and that all add personality to a composition. I show you how to add some of these to the canvas in the *Calavera* project (page 30).

NOTE: Milagros and Hojalatas

Milagros are small metal charms that are traditionally used on shrines or carried for luck. *Hojalatas* are larger folk art aluminum or tin ornaments from Mexico.

Some years ago, my friend Purna brought back a bag of tiny mirrors from India and then taught me how to stitch them onto fabric using the Simplified Shisha Stitch (page 8). Before stitching the mirrors to the canvas, glue them down so they won't slide around as you stitch. For tiny mirrors, a swipe of a glue stick works. For bigger mirrors, I use a drop of craft glue. Always wait until the mirrors are stable before stitching.

ACRYLIC MEDIUMS

Traditionally, acrylic mediums are used for enhancing acrylic paintings, but they can be used to create an embroidered art piece on canvas, too. Here are some of the mediums I have used on my canvases.

Crackle Medium

Crackle medium will give the canvas a cracked or peeling effect. Crackle medium is an easy two- to three-step process. The canvas should be crackled before stitching. The residue is light and can be effortlessly stitched through.

Crackle medium

Mica Flake Mediums

Mica is a pearly mineral that has a glittery effect. The mica flake mediums come in pearl (silver), black, and gold. A sharp needle will usually pierce through a light layer, but do a test first to see how manageable it is for you.

Mica flake gels

Iridescent Medium

Iridescent medium also contains the mineral mica, but here it is a liquid that is meant to be added to acrylic paint to produce a shiny, metallic effect. Applied as a paint, it is easy to stitch through.

Iridescent medium

Glass Bead Gel and Granular Gel

These mediums contain glass, which catches the light and creates texture. They can be added to paint. They may be used over or under the paint. They won't be easy to stitch through. I give hints on applying these mediums in the Butterfly project (page 36).

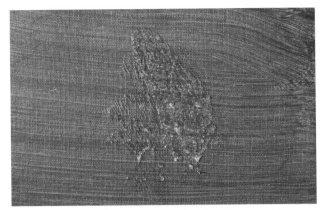

This is a clear gel that is composed of tiny glass marbles.

This clear gel creates a crushed-glass look.

Pumice Gel

Pumice has a sandy, rocky appearance and can be purchased in fine through supercoarse variations. It is definitely too hard to pierce with a needle, but it may be used on paper, fabrics, and canvas.

Pumice gel

String Gel and Clear Tar Gel

These have slightly different names but produce the same result. String gels have a thick, gooey texture and may be blended with paint. This gel is for dripping thick strands or globs onto a canvas. It is difficult to stitch through, but it may be used on papers, fabrics, and canvas.

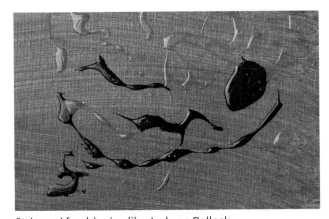

String gel for dripping like Jackson Pollock

PROJECTS

Start with a Heart

This simple project is a basic construction of art on canvas using one piece of paper and one piece of fabric, plus stitching. A soft paper such as mulberry, rice, or lokta is preferable, but most other papers will also work. Test your glue stick and craft glue on a scrap of the paper you are thinking of using. Look to see if the glue causes the paper to warp, creates stains, or causes colors printed on the paper to bleed.

Materials

STRETCHED CANVAS:
12˝ × 12˝ (30.5 cm × 30.5 cm)
*Note: Protect the sides and edges
with masking tape.*

GLUE STICK

CRAFT GLUE

SCISSORS

LIGHTWEIGHT COTTON FABRIC:
12˝ × 12˝ (30.5 cm × 30.5 cm) for heart

NEEDLES

BLACK YARN OR OTHER FIBER

DECORATIVE PAPER: 10˝ × 10˝
(25.4 cm × 25.4 cm) for background

Trim to 9¾˝ × 9¾˝ (24.8 cm × 24.8 cm).
*This will leave a little space between the
edge of the paper and the wood to stitch
or attach the borders of the piece.*

DECORATIVE/GLITTERY DUCT TAPE:
For edges

CARD STOCK: For making template

TIP ‖ *For hints on
adding variations to this
project, see Heart Project
Variations (page 27)*

HEART 1

*Make a template from the Heart pattern (page 60)
of your choosing. Trace the template onto fabric and
cut it out.*

1. Attach the decorative paper to the canvas with a
glue stick.

2. Cover the back of the fabric heart with an even
coat of glue from the glue stick. Position the heart
on the paper, and, with your fingers, press out any
air bumps so the fabric lies flat on the paper.

3. Use a running stitch to outline the heart, stitching
inside the heart.

4. Once the running stitches outline the heart, go back and connect the running stitches with the double running stitch.

5. Stem stitch around the heart, moving toward the edge of the fabric, until the edge is covered by the stitching.

6. Add a border to cover the edge of the paper. I added strips of glittery duct tape along the edge of the composition, covering the edges of the paper. Use 1 strip for each side and then strips for the top and bottom.

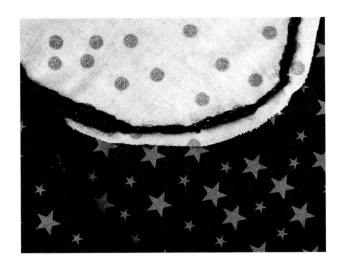

Heart Project Variations

Here are some variations using paper and fabric on canvas.

1

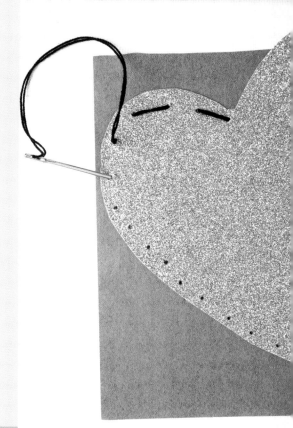

2

3

1. Paper on paper with a minimally stitched outline is a simple way to show off pretty art papers.

2. Punch holes in glittery paper; otherwise, pulling a needle upward through the underside of the canvas and poking holes with the needle pushes the paper up and looks ragged. Alternately, use a whipstitch, coming up just outside the paper and pushing the needle down into the paper.

3. Paper on paper with stitched borders. I glued scraps of the rich-looking music paper with a strong, permanent tacky glue stick, and stitched a heart around it.

I cut multiple hearts from a paper I had earlier decorated with alcohol ink. The paper was not pliable or easy to stitch on. To make this work, I glued each heart to a softer paper. See the pink construction paper on the unattached heart? I attached the heart to the canvas with a glue stick and stitched only on the softer pink paper.

Filled-in heart. Instead of using fabric or paper to create a heart in this composition, I stitched in the entire heart to match the stitching on the edges of this canvas.

Paper with card stock on fabric. Here is a paper on fabric with thick glittery card stock. I used a thick craft glue, evenly applied to the pieces of card stock.

Embroidery first, background second. I embroidered the heart straight onto the canvas with no paper or fabric background in place. I picked, cut, and placed a variety of fabric and papers around the heart. After gluing them on the canvas, I selected some yarns to stitch the items into place and then to fill the empty or negative spaces on the canvas. When completed, I added the bird with craft glue.

Calavera

Embroidering a *calavera*—a Day of the Dead sugar skull—and embellishing it with gems, charms, mirrors, and other goodies will result in a very festive canvas.

Materials

STRETCHED CANVAS:
12″ × 12″ (30.5 cm × 30.5 cm)
Note: Protect the sides and edges with masking tape.

DECORATIVE PAPER OR FABRIC:
10″ × 10″ (25.4 cm × 25.4 cm)

GLUE STICK

EMBELLISHMENTS: Such as charms, *milagros,* **folk-art pieces, mirrors, sequins,** *hojalatas,* **and gems**

CRAFT OR JEWEL GLUE

SCISSORS

NEEDLES

YARN OR OTHER FIBER

CARD STOCK: For making template

TIPS

For hints on adding variations to this project, see Calavera Project Variations (page 33).

For instructions on stitching mirrors and sequins, see Stitching on Canvas (page 6).

For an array of embellishments to consider using, see Elements of Inspiration (page 18).

For purchasing milagros *and hojalatas, see Resources for Embellishments (page 63).*

CALAVERA 1

Make two paper templates from the Calavera pattern (page 61) of your choosing. One will be attached to the canvas, and the other is for any notes you'd like to refer to as you create.

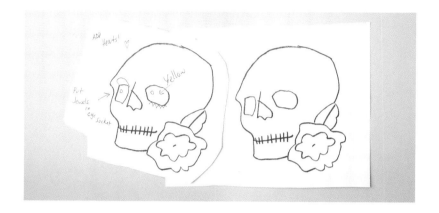

1. Choose how you will create the background, whether with paper or fabric or by leaving it plain. As with the *Start with a Heart* project (page 25), if you choose a paper or fabric background, cut the piece to 9¾″ × 9¾″ (24.8 cm × 24.8 cm) square. You may also leave the background plain to fill in the negative space with stitching later. For this canvas, I chose a soft decorative paper to use as my background. I used a glue stick to attach it to the canvas.

Apply glue stick on the back of the paper and center it on the canvas.

2. Place the paper template(s) and embellishments on the canvas and move them around until the composition pleases you. I've added a couple of small butterflies in addition to the *calavera*. Take a picture to refer to when you have decided on where the items will be placed.

With a glue stick, glue the paper template(s) where you want on the surface of the canvas.

3. With the paper template(s) fully adhered to the canvas, stitch along the outlines using a stem or running stitch.

4. Fill in the tiniest areas on the paper template(s) with satin stitches.

5. Add your choice of embellishments as you go. Use a craft or jewel glue to attach some charms, *milagros*, and folk-art pieces. Instructions on adding mirrors and sequins can be found in Stitching on Canvas (page 6).

Be sure any gems are dry and fully adhered before continuing. The primary focus of the composition I'm creating is the *calavera*. I've decided to add a *hojalata* Señor to make a little story on my canvas. After finishing with embroidering the *calavera* and butterflies, I'm ready to add El Señor to the canvas with jewel glue.

I placed Señor on the canvas in relation to where the *calavera*'s gaze is upon him.

6. Stitch the borders of your composition.

To finish the canvas, I stitched a border along the edges and added a few gems with jewel glue.

Calavera Project Variations

Here are some variations for this project, including a few embellishments that were introduced in Elements of Inspiration (page 18).

1. This canvas includes sequins, scrapbook embellishments with *milagros*, and hand-painted yarn on a velvet background. The velvet was a bit tricky to start with—very stretchy and hard to keep flat. After gluing it with a glue stick, I made running stitches along the sides to keep it taut for stitching. Those stitches are under the green chenille yarn along the border. I filled in the skull with a hand-painted yarn, using a satin stitch. The flowers, which were found among scrapbooking embellishments at a local craft store, along with the two *milagros* in the butterflies have been attached with jewel glue. The butterflies have sequins on the wings, *milagros* in the centers, and pink yarn.

2. I created this canvas by choosing an elaborate pattern for the background from a clip art book. I used my printer to copy and enlarge the design to fit into the 10″ × 10″ (25.4 cm × 25.4 cm) area within the canvas. The *calavera* features beaded sequins.

Clip art images can be found online or at bookstores.

I used a glue stick to attach the back of the image to the front of the canvas. I copied a *calavera* from my patterns and glued it in the center of the clip art image.

1. **Inspiration!** I was poking through a local craft store when a package of charms caught my attention. It brought back memories of the first job I had. I was fourteen years old and was hired to hand sew hems and details, such as sequins and beads, on opera gowns made by a local dressmaker. Madame McDaniel, the couturier, had came from Paris and her clients were very wealthy. It was exciting to go with Madame McDaniel to see her clients at their mansions and estates near San Francisco. I knew I had to honor that memory, and so I purchased these charms.

2. To convey the energy of my dear former employer, I stitched a little Eiffel Tower on the right top corner.

3. Here we have a length of ribbon, Mylar origami paper, glittery card stock, a fabric *calavera*, and a background filled with random beige floss. I started by cutting a piece of fabric that would be large enough to contain the skull pattern I chose. I glued the fabric to the canvas (design side up). Instead of gluing a paper copy of the skull pattern to the fabric, I held it in place and stitched only on the outlines of the eye sockets and nose cavity. Slowly and carefully, I tugged at the paper pattern until it came off. Do this gently, or the stitches may also come out and rip the canvas. A slightly damp sponge will soften the paper. After anchoring the skull, then completing the stitching in the nasal cavity and eye sockets, I glued down bits of the shiny origami paper and ribbon. I wrote "Couturier" on an unattached piece of gold glittery card stock. I stitched over the letters with embroidery floss and then attached it to the canvas with craft glue. Before adding the charms, I still needed to finish the remaining empty space on the background of the piece. I remembered hand hemming dozens of beige-colored silk things during my time with Madame McDaniel. I happened to have on hand a box of random shades of beige, and I filled in the canvas.

I've been stitching *calaveras* for a few years now. My very favorite item to add in the eye sockets are mirrors. I like that a viewer, on close inspection of my canvases, may be reflected in those eye sockets. (For instructions on how to add mirrors to your canvas, refer to Simplified Shisha Stitch, page 8.) This canvas also has large star-shaped beads. When beads are large and heavy, glue them on the canvas with jewel glue. Jewel glue will dry quicker than craft glue. The gold glitter dots with adhesive backs can be found at the craft store. I actually peeled the ones seen here from a party invitation, then refreshed the glue to add them here. I'm a recycler!

Milagros are small metal charms that are traditionally used on shrines or carried for luck. There's a variety of these charms, which are meant to be symbols. A dog *milagro* may mean loyalty. If you look carefully, you will find a *milagro* for anything. In this canvas, I positioned, then filled in the *calavera* first. I then stitched in a little flower and glued each *milagro* to the canvas with jewel glue. I used a satin stitch in random directions to create the yellow background, covering the attachment piece of each *milagro* under the yarn.

Folk art aluminum or tin ornaments from Mexico are called *hojalatas*. They are found in shops, and there are also online sources where you may purchase them. In the center of this canvas is a *hojalata* sun symbolizing good times ahead for the happy *calaveras* couple. I glued the sun in place with jewel glue. I drew the flowery shapes and heart directly on this canvas. I added iridescent paper triangles to represent bodies for the *calaveras*. I attached the *calavera* patterns above the iridescent paper and stitched over them. When the skulls were completely embroidered, I decorated them with beaded sequins. I filled in the background with black yarn and an orange and red border.

Butterfly

Here's a project for those that like sparkle with their stitching. In this one project, the edges of the canvas were left without tape, since unlike stitching, painted treatments can completely cover the canvas.

Materials

STRETCHED CANVAS: 12″ × 12″ (30.5 cm × 30.5 cm)
Note: Protect the sides only with masking tape.

ACRYLIC PAINT: One color of your choosing

IRIDESCENT MEDIUM

SMALL SPONGE: I cut a piece from a regular-size all-purpose sponge.

CLEAN PLASTIC WRAP

EITHER GLASS BEAD GEL OR CLEAR GRANULAR GEL

SPATULA, PALETTE KNIFE, OR DISPOSABLE PLASTIC KNIFE

PLASTIC SPOON

CARD STOCK: For making template

USUAL STITCHING MATERIALS

CRYSTAL FINE WHITE GLITTER: *Optional*, **for extra bling. We will use only a tiny bit.**

TIP || *For hints on adding variations to this project, see Butterfly Project Variations (page 40).*

BUTTERFLY 1

Refer to the basics chapters as needed.

Make two paper templates from the Butterfly pattern (page 62) of your choosing. One will be attached to the canvas, and the other is for any notes you'd like to refer to as you create.

1. Combine about 1 teaspoon (4.9 mL) of acrylic paint with roughly 2 tablespoons (29.6 mL) of iridescent medium.

The iridescent medium adds a pearly appearance to the paint.

2. Use the sponge to apply the paint mixture all over the canvas.

3. As the paint is still wet, add extra texture by tapping the canvas with a balled-up piece of plastic wrap.

Any bit of plastic wrap will work. Be sure it's clean. Before continuing on, let the paint dry completely.

4. Position the butterfly paper template into place. To keep the paper template from shifting, baste it with a simple X, a few inches (about 8 cm) long, to make the stitches easily removable. Keep snippers nearby, because the stitches holding the paper template in place will need to be removed right after applying the gels.

Items at the ready for this part of the project, including a clean piece of sponge in case of any drips.

5. Drop spoonfuls of the gel onto the canvas. I begin with the corners.

Use a spatula, palette knife, or a plastic knife, not a paintbrush, for this. Work the gel up to the paper pattern. It's fine to get some on the paper, but be sure it won't seal the area underneath.

Circle toward the paper pattern with the gel.

6. Once the gel is evenly spread out on the canvas, spoon some gel along the edges of the pattern.

Smooth out the gel along the pattern's edges so it blends with the gel on the rest of the canvas.

7. After all the gel is on the canvas, sprinkle the crystal fine glitter on the gel. Snip the basting thread. Pull all the basting thread away from underneath the canvas. Remove the paper template from the canvas.

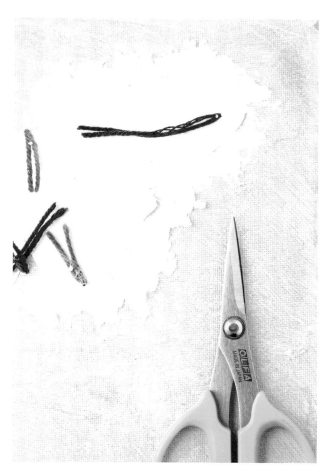

Snip the threads before the gel dries.

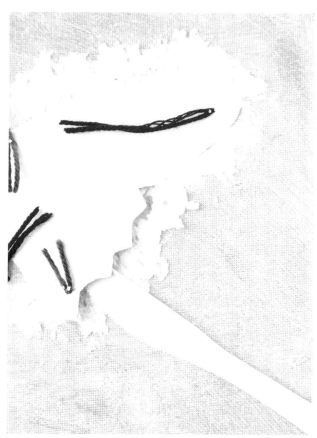

If the pattern is sticking to the canvas, loosen and lift up the edge with a knife or edge of the snippers.

8. Before filling in the butterfly area with stitching, let the canvas completely dry. It may take overnight for the gel to set. The gel is opaque when wet but will be clear when dry. If a little gel gets under the paper template, you may be able to scrape it off, but just a bit is usually pliable enough to embroider through.

9. Embroider the butterfly as desired.

I used warm colors in the butterfly to contrast the very cool aqua background.

Butterfly Project Variations

In Elements of Inspiration (page 18), there are descriptions of a variety of acrylic mediums. Here are embroidered canvases that include using some of these mediums.

Here, glass bead gel is all over the place, mixed with glitter in some areas and painted over with periwinkle acrylic paint in others. The background was first coated with an acrylic metallic blue paint. The paper template then was basted to the surface of the canvas. Some glass bead medium was applied. While the canvas was still wet with gel, I added some gold glitter. I plopped a bit of periwinkle acrylic paint in a few small areas before letting the canvas completely dry and then did the stitching in the butterfly.

String gel was mixed with black acrylic paint to create the background of this canvas. I began with a coat of gold acrylic paint on the canvas. After the paint had dried, I basted the butterfly paper template to the canvas. I mixed a spoonful of black acrylic paint with string gel per manufacturer's instructions and then used a plastic knife to scoop up some of the mixture and drip it over the canvas.

There's no need to baste the paper template to the canvas when using a crackle medium background because the crackle medium, when dried, leaves a thin film that won't interfere with stitching on the canvas. Apply the medium to the canvas per the manufacturer's instructions before stitching. The gel can be applied over a base coat of acrylic paint. They must be completely dry before adding a top coat of a different color acrylic paint.

I traced the butterfly paper template directly on the canvas multiple times for a kaleidoscope of butterflies. I then drew the designs on the wings. With a plastic knife, I added extracoarse pumice gel into the areas of the butterfly bodies. I found using a toothpick or a needle was helpful in pushing stray pumice pieces into place. The pumice gel needs time to dry before continuing to stitch. I didn't add color to the gel, though you may do this by mixing the gel with paint. Untinted pumice gel stays a grayish, oatmeal color when dried.

Tips on Showing Your Art

FINISHING THE BACK

Once the front of your canvas is complete, the time has come to detail the back. Covering the back of the canvas keeps dust out, helps the stitches stay tight, and makes your art piece presentable for display. Materials for finishing the back of the canvas and for adding wire are listed in Starting Out: Notes on Supplies (page 12).

1. Remove the masking tape you used to protect the exposed canvas. Lay the canvas front side down on a clean, level surface.

2. Cut an 11½″ × 11½″ (29.2 cm × 29.2 cm) square of package or butcher paper.

3. Run a line of glue along the exposed staples.

4. Center the paper square on the canvas back, covering or getting close to covering the glue and staples.

5. Wait until the glue has dried. Cover and secure the edges of the paper with masking tape, one side and strip of tape at a time.

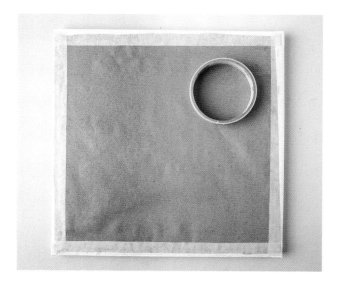

6. If there is a puffiness to the paper, very lightly tap a very slightly damp sponge across the paper. This helps to reduce puffs.

WIRING

Start with a clean, level area to work on.

1. Before laying the canvas front side down, check that the top of the image is still at the top.

2. Measure 4˝ (10.2 cm) down from the top of the canvas. Mark the measurement with a pen on the stretcher bar area. Repeat on the opposite stretcher bar.

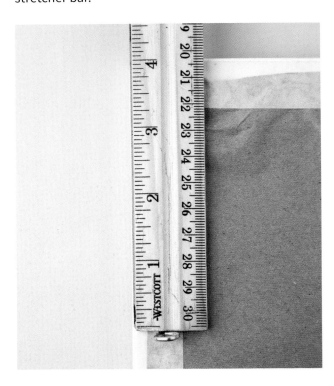

3. Manually screw in the eye screws where you have made the pen marks.

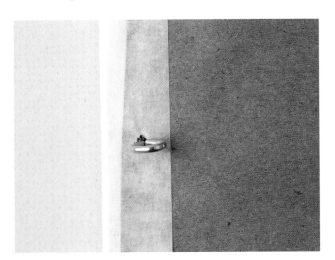

4. Pass the wire through both eye screws.

5. Knot the wire in one eye.

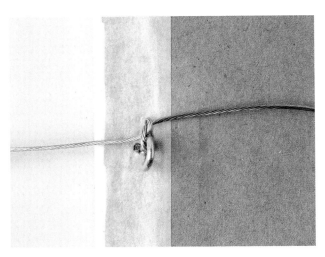

6. Carefully pull the wire tight and firm as you knot the wire to the second eye screw. Wrap the ends of the wire around the tight wire and tape the ends. Congratulations! Your canvas is ready to be displayed.

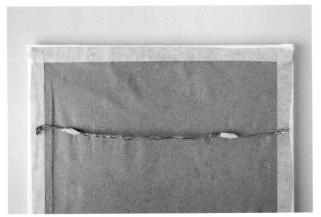

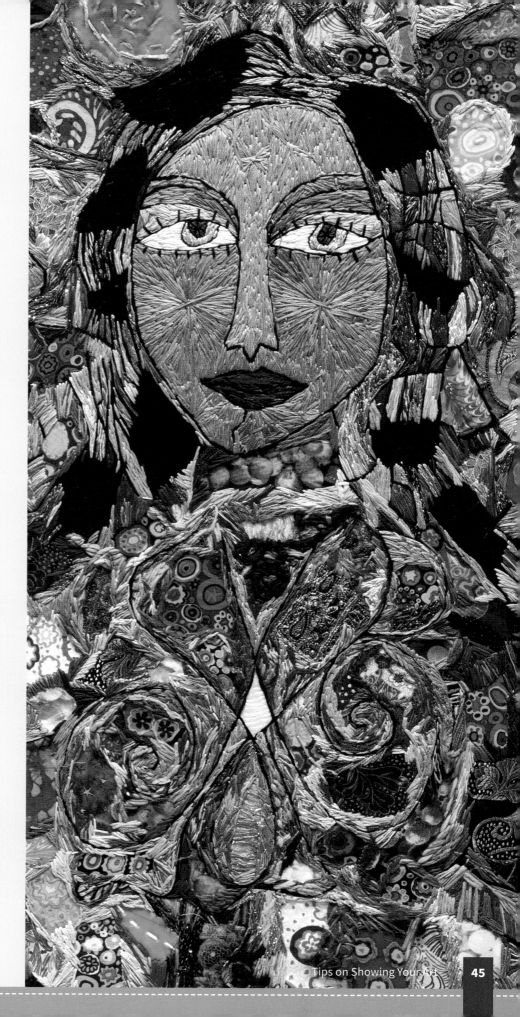

STITCHING IS ART

Stitching is art, and like any other art form, it deserves a place in exhibits, galleries, and museums. Are you ready to give exhibiting a go?

Look into your local art guilds that support mixed media, fiber, textile, and surface design art. These clubs and guilds often are contacted to arrange displays in libraries, city halls, and fairs. I am a member of numerous art organizations. One of my favorite groups arranges exhibits in neighborhood bars, coffee shops, and restaurants around San Francisco. I've sold my embroidered canvases at a craft brewery, a bowling alley, and a wellness center. Ask around at local, independently owned framing and art materials stores. Ask the staff to find out who and where your local artists' organization is. In my experience, any independent art store staff member will know what's happening in local artist circles.

Thank you for buying this book and trying out these methods. Believe in yourself and go for it! Happy creating!!

Cheers,

—*Irene*

Gallery and Student Pieces

The following works are by the author, except where noted.

Inspire, 12″ × 12″
(30.5 cm × 30.5 cm)

Mariposa, 12″ × 12″
(30.5 cm × 30.5 cm)

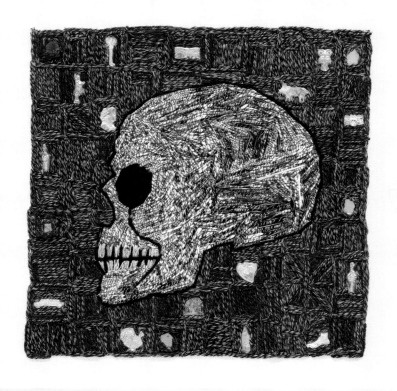

Sideways, 12″ × 12″
(30.5 cm × 30.5 cm)

Hearts and Cards, 12″ × 12″
(30.5 cm × 30.5 cm)

String Gel Heart, 12″ × 12″
(30.5 cm × 30.5 cm)

Milagros, 12″ × 12″
(30.5 cm × 30.5 cm)

Fiesta Skull, 12″ × 12″
(30.5 cm × 30.5 cm)

Always Dreaming
by Sasha Schlesinger,
12″ × 12″
(30.5 cm × 30.5 cm)

Butterflies Rising
by Purna Hegde, 12″ × 12″
(30.5 cm × 30.5 cm)

Polka Dot Love
by Linda Leibovich, 12″ × 12″
(30.5 cm × 30.5 cm)

Doily Heart by Linda Leibovich, 12″ × 12″ (30.5 cm × 30.5 cm)

Shulamit, 30″ × 40″ (76.2 cm × 101.6 cm)

Twinkle Cat, 12˝ × 12˝
(30.5 cm × 30.5 cm)

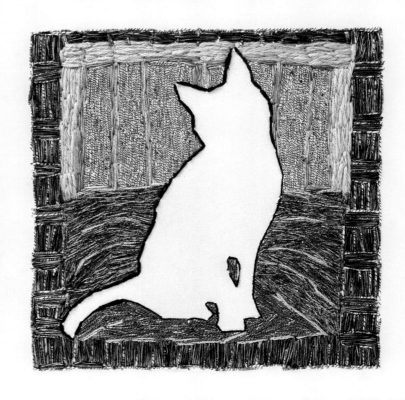

Snowball, 12˝ × 12˝
(30.5 cm × 30.5 cm)

Mermaid Skull, 18˝ × 24˝ (45.7 cm × 61 cm)

Estelle Coy Ojos Verde, 20˝ × 20˝ (50.8 cm × 50.8 cm)

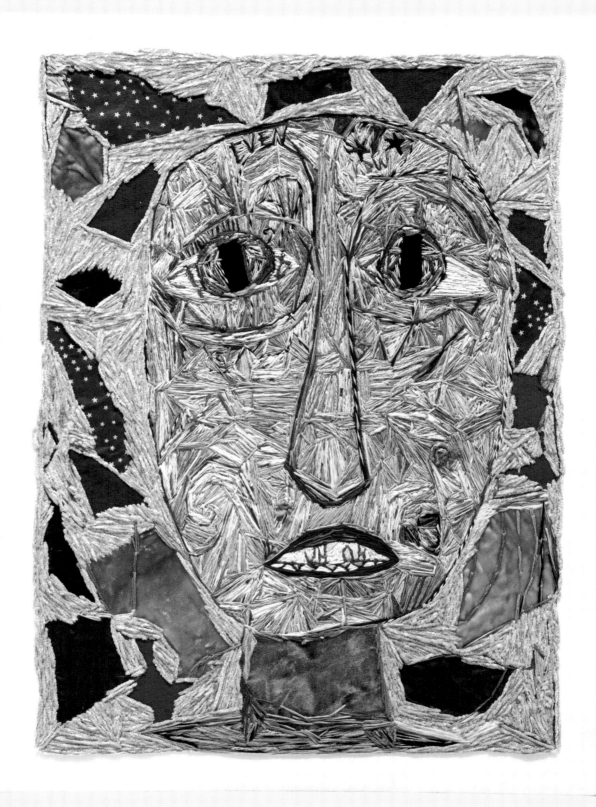

Mr. Uh Oh, 22˝ × 28˝ (55.9 cm × 71.1 cm)

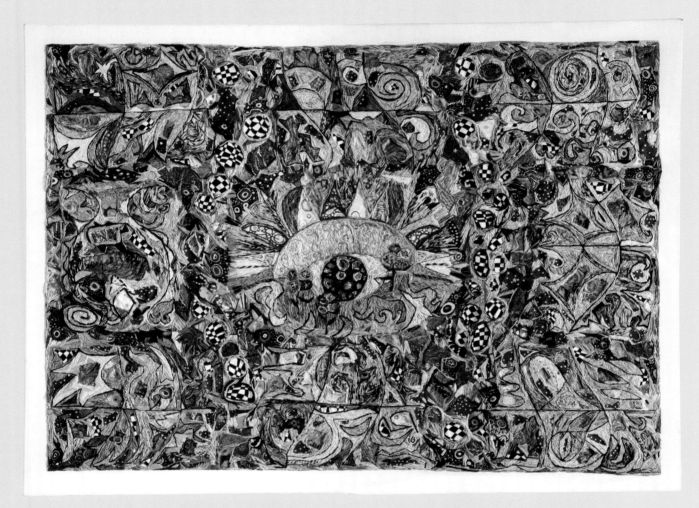

Safe Space, 48″ × 36″ (121.9 cm × 91.4 cm)

If Nothing Ever Changed, 12″ × 12″ (30.5 cm × 30.5 cm)

Project Patterns

Here are simple patterns for use on 12″ (20.5 cm) canvases.

Start with a Heart

Big heart

Start with a Heart

(page 24)

Start with a Heart

Little heart

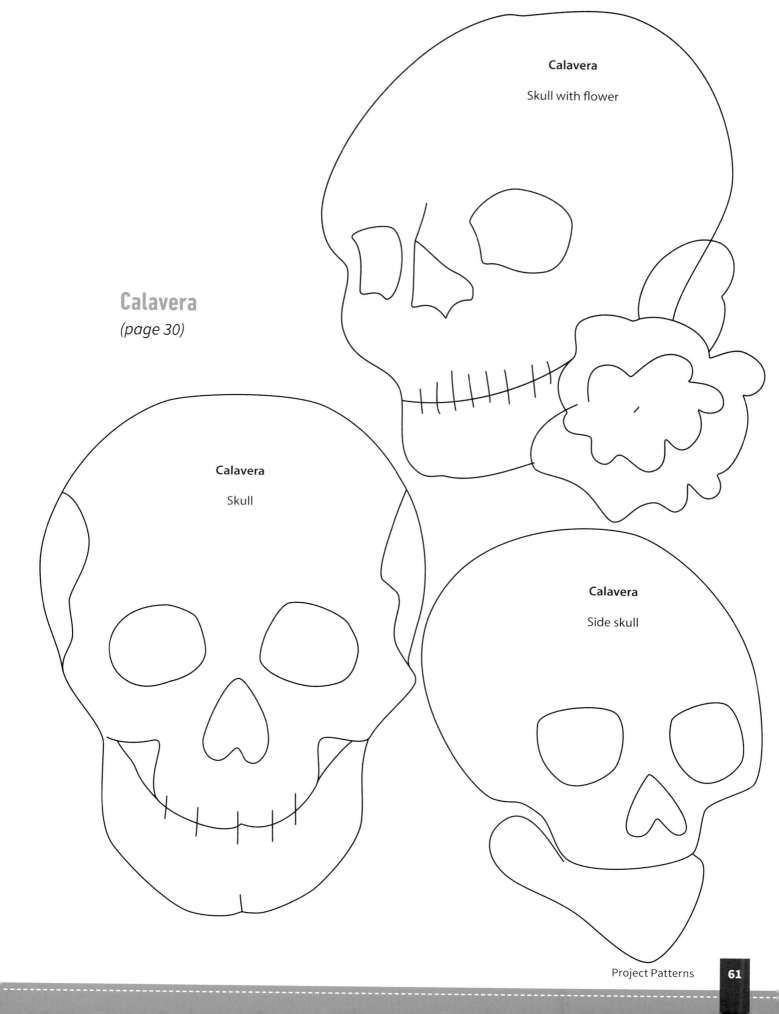

Calavera

Skull with flower

Calavera

(page 30)

Calavera

Skull

Calavera

Side skull

Butterfly

(page 36)

Butterfly

Big butterfly

Butterfly

Little butterfly

About the Author

IRENE SCHLESINGER is an emerging San Francisco Bay Area artist. Irene was taught how to stitch by her grandmother as soon as she could hold a needle. She attended art classes at California College of Arts and Crafts, San Francisco State University, and Stanford University. Inspired by Folk, Surreal, Expressionist, and Outsider artists, vibrant colors, patterns, and textures are expressed in Irene's embroidered canvases and mixed medium panels.

Visit Irene online and follow on social media!

Blog: artfulembroidery.blog

Website: ireneschlesingerartwork.com

Instagram: @irenie_artwork

Pinterest: @irenie_artworks

Facebook: /irenembroiders • /ireneschlesingerartwork

Photo by Scott Schlesinger

RESOURCES FOR EMBELLISHMENTS

I try to find and purchase from my local shops, but sometimes one must look online. Here are a few independent merchants that carry wares online.

For a beautiful selection of papers from around the world:

Two Hands Paperie   *twohandspaperie.com*

For kraft-tex—paper that looks like leather and can be stitched like fabric, and comes in an array of colors:

C&T Publishing   *ctpub.com*

For *hojalatas* and *milagros*:

Casa Bonampak   *casabonampak.com*

Want even more creative content?

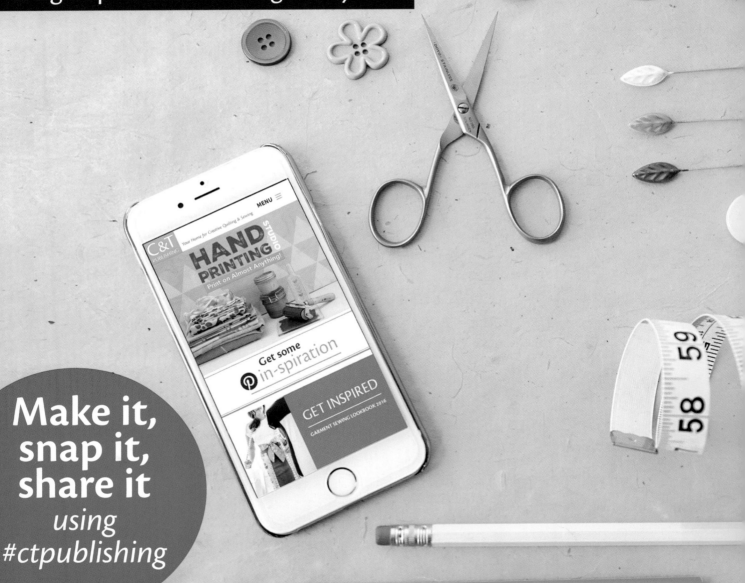

Make it, snap it, share it
using #ctpublishing